Children of the World

Turkey

For a free color catalog describing Gareth Stevens' list of high-quality children's books, call 1-800-341-3569 (USA) or 1-800-461-9120 (Canada).

For their help in the preparation of *Children of the World: Turkey*, the editors gratefully thank Employment and Immigration Canada, Ottawa, Ont.; the US Immigration and Naturalization Service, Washington, DC; and the United States Department of State, Bureau of Public Affairs, Office of Public Communication, Washington, DC, for unencumbered use of material in the public domain.

Library of Congress Cataloging-in-Publication Data

Tozuka, Takako.
   Turkey.

   (Children of the world)
   Includes index.
   Summary: Presents the life of an eleven-year-old girl and her family living in Nevsehir, the largest city in the Cappadocia area of Turkey, describing her home and school, daily activities, amusements, and some of the customs and celebration of her country.
   1. Turkey—Juvenile literature. [1. Family life—Turkey. 2. Turkey—Social life and customs] I. Sukup, Don. II. Title. III. Series.
DR418.T69 1989   956.1   88-32745
ISBN 1-55532-851-2

North American edition first published in 1989 by

Gareth Stevens Children's Books
RiverCenter Building, Suite 201
1555 North RiverCenter Drive
Milwaukee, Wisconsin 53212, USA

This work was originally published in shortened form consisting of section 1 only. Photographs and original text copyright © 1989 by Takako Tozuka. First and originally published by Kaisei-sha Publishing Co., Ltd., Tokyo. World English rights arranged with Kaisei-sha Publishing Co., Ltd. through Japan Foreign-Rights Centre.

Copyright this format © 1989 by Gareth Stevens, Inc.
Additional material and maps copyright © 1989 by Gareth Stevens, Inc.

Series editor: Rhoda Irene Sherwood
Research editor: Scott Enk
Map design: Sheri Gibbs

Printed in the United States of America

2 3 4 5 6 7 8 9 95 94 93 92 91 90

Children of the World

Turkey

Photography by
Takako Tozuka

Edited by
Scott Enk,
Rita Reitci,
Rhoda Sherwood, &
Donald Sukup

Gareth Stevens Children's Books
MILWAUKEE

. . . a note about *Children of the World*:

The children of the world live in fishing towns and urban centers, on islands and in mountain valleys, on sheep ranches and fruit farms. This series follows one child in each country through the pattern of his or her life. Candid photographs show the children with their families, at school, at play, and in their communities. The text describes the dreams of the children and, often through their own words, tells how they see themselves and their lives.

Each book also explores events that are unique to the country in which the child lives, including festivals, religious ceremonies, and national holidays. The *Children of the World* series does more than tell about foreign countries. It introduces the children of each country and shows readers what it is like to be a child in that country.

. . . and about *Turkey*:

Nurdan, an 11-year-old girl from Nevshehir, lives with her parents and two sisters in a small town on the Anatolian plateau. Like her sisters, she is a good student and, like them, she plans to go to the university to train for a profession. But she is also an ordinary girl who loves to visit her grandmother, play with friends in the neighborhood, and giggle with her sisters.

To enhance this book's value in libraries and classrooms, comprehensive reference sections include up-to-date information about Turkey's geography, demographics, language, currency, education, culture, industry, and natural resources. *Turkey* also features a bibliography, research topics, activity projects, and discussions of such subjects as Istanbul, the country's history, language, political system, and ethnic and religious composition.

The living conditions and experiences of children in Turkey vary according to economic, environmental, and ethnic circumstances. The reference sections help bring to life for young readers the diversity and richness of the culture and heritage of Turkey. Of particular interest are discussions of Turkey's architecture and its long and exciting history.

CONTENTS

Five times each day, a voice from this mosque behind Nurdan's house calls Muslims to prayer.

LIVING IN TURKEY:
Nurdan, a Girl of the Anatolian Plateau

Meet Nurdan, an 11-year-old girl who lives with her mother and father, Mesgüre and Necati, her older sister, Handan, and her younger sister, Güldan. They live in the small city of Nevshehir on the central plateau of Turkey.

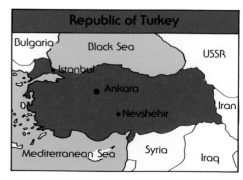

Nurdan's family: her mother, Mesgüre, Nurdan, her sister Handan, her sister Güldan, and her father, Necati.

Nurdan's father wears his policeman's uniform.
The girls wear their school uniforms.

The family has lived in Nevshehir for two years. They have a house with a kitchen, two bedrooms, and a living and dining room combined. Nearby is a mosque, their place of worship.

Nevshehir lies in a fascinating region called Cappadocia. Here weathered rock forms the shape of cones, mushrooms, or weirdly twisted poles. Centuries of erosion created this striking stone forest.

Centuries of weathering produced these strange and colorful formations of volcanic rock in central Anatolia. Some of these ancient rock dwellings are used as houses, small hotels, and even discos.

Nurdan and her family enjoy watching videos; the girls like cartoons while their parents prefer dramas about Turkey's history.

Nurdan and Her Family

After Nurdan finishes elementary school, she will enter middle school. Handan, age fifteen, will go to a *lise*, a high school. Güldan, eight, will be in third grade; she's pretty proud of herself because she did well in first grade and will skip second.

Handan does housework and takes care of her younger sisters. She thinks Güldan is a handful because she is so mischievous and such a clown. All three sisters are good-natured.

Mesgüre takes care of the home, and Necati is a policeman. When he comes home from work at 5 p.m., the family has dinner. Then he sometimes goes to the *lokanta*, or restaurant, or to the *kahvehane*, or coffee house, places where men talk or play backgammon and other games.

An older style of bathroom. Vacuuming the Turkish carpet. It's Nurdan's turn to wash dishes.

Most people in Turkey live quite modestly. In their bedroom, the girls have two beds and a mattress that they place on the floor. Because water is scarce, the family never knows when a faucet will stop flowing. So they use water carefully. They wash dishes in as little water as possible, and to flush the toilet, they pump water into the tank. The family usually jokes about these inconveniences.

Nurdan's family moves often because of Necati's work. "As soon as I've made new friends, I have to say good-bye," says Nurdan. "Still, some of my friends have to go to West Germany to get jobs, so I suppose we are lucky."

During difficult economic times, when people cannot find jobs at home, they work abroad in order to support their families.

Reading in their bedroom.

11

The refreshments disappear quickly.

The elementary-school boys portraying soldiers.

The Spring Festival

The sounds of flutes and drums resound throughout Turkey. It is April — time for the spring festivals. The people eagerly join in the many dancing contests held all over the country. Dancers wear bright scarves, colorful clothing with gold ornaments, and baggy pants gathered at the ankle.

Nurdan loves to dance, too. Every day after school she goes to a folk-dancing class. The three sisters began lessons together at the cultural arts school, but only Nurdan finished the two-year course and earned her certificate. The school also teaches folk music, lace making, and embroidery.

Turkish people love their ancient dances. In this one, dancers carry wooden spoons.

A contest for young girls — Little Miss Turkey.

Musicians play folk music on traditional instruments.

Today they celebrate Tourism Day. Nurdan joins a group from her school. Dressed in gorgeous clothes, she is excited but nervous, too, because so many people will be watching. The musicians begin, and Nurdan hears the sounds of the rhythmic drums, the wood-winds, and the *kemençe*. This instrument is like a mandolin but is as large as a cello.

At last the dance is over. Everyone applauds. Nurdan and her friends rush to the refreshment tables, for they are very hungry after all that activity. The women have set out for them apples, yogurt drink, cheese, and *nan*, a kind of bread made from a dough of flour and eggs.

Nurdan goes to the beach on the Black Sea with her aunt and her cousins, Nurhan and Kubra. Nurdan is not very good at swimming, so she helps five-year-old Kubra build a sand castle.

Summer Vacation by the Black Sea

In May, the schools close for the summer. They will not open again until September, so the children have more than three months of vacation. Every year, Nurdan and her family go to Samsun, a large port city on the Black Sea. Nurdan's beloved grandmother lives there and Mesgüre grew up there. When she was seventeen, she met her future husband, who was boarding in the house across the street. They were soon married. Nurdan was born in Samsun too.

Nurdan's mother has brothers and sisters who still live in Samsun, so the family also visits them. At the beginning of vacation, Grandmother comes to Nevshehir to help the family move for the summer. She and Mesgüre and the children set out happily for the coast. Necati's vacation is not until August. He will join his family in Samsun then.

Nevshehir, on the plateau, is dry, with little greenery. But at Samsun are the sparkling blue sea with the wide sandy beach, movie theaters and a large amusement park, toy shops and dress shops. Nurdan can hardly wait to get to busy, bustling Samsun.

Grandfather runs a spice shop in the middle of the city with Nurdan's uncle. Right next door is her aunt's ice cream shop. Nurdan visits the spice shop every day. Then she has an ice cream cone at her aunt's shop. At lunch time, all the relatives gather at Grandmother's house to eat. The happy days pass quickly.

Shopping on the main street of Samsun.

At the amusement park.

A summer wedding in Samsun.

Carrying a mat, Nurdan is off to the beach.

Buying bread at the baker's shop.

Last Days in Samsun

Family ties are very important in Turkey. On weekends, Nurdan eats dinner at Kubra's house. Kubra's father is Mesgüre's younger brother. Nurdan looks forward to all the bustle and chatter when relatives gather for meals.

Nurdan's family had gone home two weeks before, but she was allowed to stay behind with Grandmother. Actually, she would like to live in Samsun and go to middle school. Her parents aren't so sure. Father said they would think about it and decide at the end of summer.

The toy store. There are none in Nevshehir.

Playing in the green park behind Grandmother's house.

The family gathers at Uncle's house. They have *pide*, a kind of bread, and *çay*, tea.

When September arrives, Nurdan's neighbors from Nevshehir come to take Nurdan home. Kenan is twenty and his wife, Nursel, is only seventeen. They tell Nurdan that her father has decided that she is to live at home and attend a local middle school. Both Nurdan and her grandmother are disappointed. They like each other's company and were looking forward to a whole year with each other.

With Grandfather at the spice shop.

Nurdan helps make the beds.

Making Nurdan's favorite, *köfte*, or lamb hamburgers.

Grandmother making pastry for baklava.

Nurdan's last dinner in Samsun.

Baklava, layers of pastry and nuts covered with syrup.

On Nurdan's last evening in Samsun, she helps Grandmother make *baklava*, a traditional sweet pastry. When Grandfather and Uncle return from the spice shop, everyone eats dinner — *yaprak dolmasi*, rice and raisins wrapped in vine leaves, with green pickled peppers.

After tea, it is time to leave. Nurdan kisses Grandfather good-bye. As she hugs her grandmother, she begins crying. Grandmother is sad, too. But she tries to make Nurdan feel better and reminds her that they'll be together the next summer.

Opposite: Saying good-bye brings tears.

18

A whole household moves by bus.

The Journey Home

The bus swoops past sleeping towns at 60 miles an hour (100 kph). Most of the buses are high-performance vehicles that are faster than the trains. So the bus is a popular form of transportation.

When the threesome board the bus, an employee of the bus line sprays their hands with cologne. The whole bus soon fills with the scent of roses.

Late that night, the bus arrives in Ankara. The travelers sleepily enter the waiting room. A fog of tobacco smoke fills the air, and people wander around carrying bundles and luggage. Nurdan, Nursel, and Kenan go to the food stall to get some tea and cheese sandwiches.

The sun rises as they board the bus to Nevshehir. Cruising through a desolate landscape of bare hills, the bus passes sheep and chickens, and dogs that amble down the country road. Farmers go to their fields leading heavily laden donkeys. Soon the threesome will be home. The journey has taken more than fourteen hours.

Ready to board.

The bus travels through a plain that is flat as far as the eye can see.

This bus line serves water to the passengers.

The bus terminal food stand is open 24 hours a day.

The covers of the textbooks are thin, so children cover them with plastic for protection.

Nurdan's report card.
She earned good grades.

Nurdan's certificate from
the school of cultural arts.

Nurdan's Polish pen pal
sends her beautiful pictures.

Starting School

School could not begin because there weren't enough textbooks printed. Then a TV announcer informed parents that the books were in the stores. School would begin the very next day!

Mesgüre and Handan hurried to all six bookstores in Nevshehir with book lists, but all they could find were Handan's math and chemistry books and Nurdan's Turkish and history books.

This has become a common problem because Turkey has so improved health care for all that the population has increased. Schools and other institutions have not quite adjusted to this population growth. But during this temporary situation, children happily share texts until everyone has gotten one.

Mesgüre adjusts Handan's uniform.

Children crowd the stores to buy schoolbooks.

Boys in middle school have their hair cut.

Breakfast is bread, cheese, olives, and tea.

Mother braids the girls' hair every morning.

The Opening Ceremony

The family gets up unusually early, for school begins today. Handan goes to the lise with Kenan. Although he is married, he still studies at the lise.

Necati attends the opening ceremony.

Güldan walks 10 minutes to her elementary school. Nurdan will go to middle school right across the street. The school's opening ceremony starts at 8:30 a.m. Nurdan feels grown-up in a long uniform skirt and black stockings.

The opening ceremony is held before a bust of Mustafa Kemal Atatürk, hero of Turkish independence.

Nurdan's middle school is in a four-storied building.

The opening ceremony: The principal hoists the Turkish flag. The students, their parents, and the uniformed policemen all stand at attention. After singing the national anthem, they listen to the principal's speech. Then the students file into the school. Nurdan's studies will be much harder this year, so she realizes she will have more homework.

In Nurdan's English class, the teacher uses flash cards.

A Day at the Middle School

The middle school has grades six, seven, and eight. Girls are in black uniforms. Boys dress in suits and ties. Children sit three to a desk. When students raise their hands, they point one finger upward.

Nurdan has been looking forward to her foreign language class. The school offers English and German. Most students want English, but often there are not enough spaces for them, so they pick a coin out of a bag, which determines the language they will study. Nurdan has been looking forward to learning English, so she prays, "Please, God, let me get the coin for English class." When the teacher announces, "English," Nurdan leaps for joy. She is a member of class 6C.

English class is short of textbooks. So the teacher, Miss Sevcihan, holds up a flash card and says in English, "He is a doctor." This is Nurdan's first meeting with English, and she joins the other students in repeating "He is a doctor." At this stage, they probably do not understand what they are saying, but they enjoy the sounds of the language anyway.

The students have only three classes in English each week, so they often forget what they have learned in the previous class. Miss Sevcihan says she would like to use language tapes, but there is no money for them, so she uses as much English as she can in the classroom.

Another course Nurdan likes is history. Mr. Yüksel gives the history lessons. Today he talks about the founder of modern Turkey, Mustafa Kemal Atatürk. Everywhere in Turkey — in government offices, in schools, in public buildings, in parks, and in many private homes — there are pictures and statues of Atatürk.

Mr. Yüksel asks a question in history class.

Working at a small loom in domestic science class.

Coin purse, key case, glasses case, and other items made in domestic science class.

Learning to rasp wood in industrial arts class.

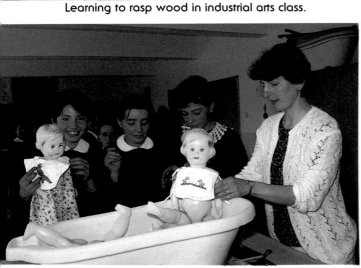
Using dolls to practice caring for babies.

After history are domestic science and industrial arts classes. Boys and girls attend both. From the time they are very young, girls learn sewing and knitting from their grand-mothers and mothers. So by middle school, they are adept at these crafts. Nurdan sees a boy knitting baby booties and nearby a girl sews a bib. They are doing well. But the boy next to her is having trouble, so Nurdan shows him a better way to hold the needle and the cloth.

In industrial arts class, students saw wood and shape it with a rasp, a coarse file. They learn to fasten wood with screws. Later, they are going to learn to work with electrical wiring, and to repair electrical devices.

In the hall is a board with photos of the top students of the year. Nurdan was a star in elementary school. Now she is determined to have her photo placed on the special bulletin board, too. School will be harder now, but she is used to studying. Her parents will be proud of her if she continues to get high marks. Mesgüre and Necati encourage the girls to get as much as possible out of their education.

Near the student pictures are many photos of Atatürk, who opened the doors to education for all of Turkey's people. He urged the nation to build new schools and universities throughout the country. Nurdan is looking forward to learning more about him in history class.

These are the year's top students.

A wall honoring Atatürk.

The Father of Modern Turkey

Early this century, Turkey was still ruled by sultans, but it had lost much of its glory and land after a series of wars. Turkey was on the losing side during World War I, so afterward the Allies prepared to divide the nation among themselves and sent troops to occupy the country.

But a Turkish general, Mustafa Kemal, rallied his army to resist the Allies. In 1922, they won, and the next year Turkey became a republic. Mustafa Kemal knew that, to stay free, his country needed a stable economy and modern attitudes. So as Turkey's first president, he reformed education, established civil and legal rights for both women and men, and encouraged the arts and sciences. For this, he was given the name Atatürk, "Father of the Turks."

Nurdan's middle-school class, 6C, has 42 students.

Atatürk's most important reform was education for all. At that time, only 10% of the people could read and write, and schools were under religious control. Atatürk replaced the difficult Arabic script with the easier Roman letters. Language experts simplified the grammar and replaced some foreign words with the original Turkish. Atatürk himself visited parks and schoolrooms to teach this new alphabet.

Soon adults and children everywhere were learning to read and write. New public schools appeared. Girls as well as boys now receive free schooling; the government encourages both to enter professions they would like and to study at universities and vocational institutes. Most of these schools are also free.

The teachers' room.

Children buying lunch at the school canteen.

Lunch and Afternoon

The bell for the lunch hour rings at 12 noon. Nurdan and most of the other students hurry out of the building. The lunch period is one hour and 15 minutes long, so there is enough time for many students to eat at home. Only a few children live so far away that they cannot go home and return during the lunch period.

Students who want to buy food at school go to the school canteen. There they can buy bread, cheese, eggs, apples, and candy. Teachers often bring their own food. After lunch, they will rest or plan lessons in the teachers' room.

Who is hiding the handkerchief?

Soccer is a popular sport with boys.

The school canteen sells supplies like note pads and pencils. But because children in Turkey are like children almost everywhere, the most popular items are candy — particularly chocolate — and gum! During breaks, the canteen also sells drinks like fruit juices or apple tea to students and teachers.

Nurdan and her father hurry home. Mother busily prepares lunch. Today it is spaghetti topped with meat and spices — one of Nurdan's favorite meals, so she asks for a second helping. Then everyone naps before beginning the afternoon.

Gradually, from the middle school across the street, come the sounds of children returning from home. Before class, they play in the schoolyard. Nurdan hurries to join them. Soon she is enjoying a game of hopscotch. Some girls begin to play "Where's the handkerchief?" And some boys start a soccer game. Soon the afternoon bell rings, the playing stops, and the children rush into school for afternoon classes.

Climbing on the bars during physical education class.

Next is math class. Nurdan pays close attention because math is not easy for her. She knows that in order to get into the university, she will need to know math very well.

Nurdan also studies Islam, the Muslim religion. Atatürk kept religious teaching out of the public schools. But 98% of the population is Muslim, and some people want religious classes for their children.

Nurdan runs to her Turkish class. The students must memorize a classic poem for the next class. By the end of the hour, she knows the first lines. Children in middle school also memorize up to ten verses of the national anthem, the "Istiklâl Marsi," or Independence March.

Then she hurries to physical education class, happy to be letting off some steam. "Our equipment has not arrived yet," the teacher announces. So everyone gets to do what they want for the day. Nurdan and some friends rush to the climbing bars and race each other to the top.

Students leave school at four o'clock.

After-school Playtime

When Nurdan gets home from school, her sisters are already there. Handan gets out of school by one o'clock because another school uses the building in the afternoon. There are no extracurricular activities after school, so she comes right home. She gets up so early for school that when she gets home, she usually flops on the sofa to take a nap.

Güldan does her homework while she waits for Nurdan to come home. The two younger sisters go to schools that do not need to share space with another school. But it is common in Turkey for children to attend classes in shifts, and shortages of school materials frequently occur. The government learns more each year, however, about how to plan for school enrollment. In the meantime, the children have learned to be generous with one another. Güldan finishes her homework and the younger sisters rush out to play before dinner.

It takes skill to roll a hoop along rapidly.

A pause in a cops-and-robbers game.

Nurdan and her friends enjoy jumping rope, although they also like to make up games such as trivia contests.

The weather is mild today, so the children play outside. They like tag, hopscotch, dodge ball, hide-and-seek, cops-and-robbers, and jumping rope. The goal is to have fun, not to trounce opponents. No player is made to feel bad. A penalty for losing a game is often something silly like a stunt — for instance, crowing like a rooster — or a teasing verse sung by the others. Adults often play games they learned as children. They, too, enjoy showing off their physical skills and fast thinking.

The Turkish people value physical activity. Boys enjoy basketball and soccer, and some even hope to join a professional team when they grow up. Sports clubs recruit adults to play on amateur teams. In wrestling, Turkey's traditional sport, athletes have won Olympic medals for their country. Males from age 15 on up train hard for the annual national wrestling championships.

Time to Study

Before dinner, Nurdan does homework. She uses part of her bookcase as a desk. Mesgüre is grateful — all three girls like to do schoolwork. She and Necati won't have money to give the girls when they leave home, so they advise them to get professions that they will enjoy and that will support them.

Nurdan loves children and plans to be a pediatrician, a doctor who specializes in children's health. Because Handan also enjoys being with children, she plans to teach in an elementary school. Güldan hasn't decided, but she thinks she wants to be a pharmacist, a person who dispenses medicines in a drugstore or hospital.

Everyone leaves in the morning at a different time, so they eat breakfast according to their own schedule. For this reason, Mesgüre wants the family to share the evening meal. After dinner, the girls help clean up. Then they play with their dolls or read for relaxation or watch television with their parents.

Nurdan's bookcase sometimes serves as a desk.

Memorizing a poem for tomorrow's class.

37

Sunday Mornings

Sunday morning! Handan prepares breakfast while Mesgüre keeps watch out of the window. Suddenly Mother puts some eggs into a bowl and rushes outside. Next to the house, neighbor women are gathering to make nan, a very thin, flat bread. They mix a dough of eggs and flour and place it on an iron plate in the oven. A delicious smell soon fills the air. Skillfully, they flip the baking bread with a stick, and soon it is done. Mesgüre gives ten eggs to the oldest woman there and asks her to make nan for her.

When Mesgüre brings in the freshly baked nan, Nurdan butters a large piece, which she spreads with cheese, tomatoes, and pickled green peppers. Then she neatly folds it up. Later she takes this with her when she goes with Nursel to help in the field where Nursel and Kenan grow tomatoes.

When they return home, Nurdan rushes to the rope swing Kenan has made. The children giggle as they push and swing one another around on this new toy.

Off to the field with Nursel from next door.

Taking turns on the swing Kenan has made.

Baking nan. Some women wear scarves, and many townspeople pray five times daily, as Islam dictates. Nurdan's mother is city-born and goes bareheaded. The family does not practice Islam strictly.

How to eat nan: 1. Butter it and put on toppings. 2. Fold it up. 3. Take a big bite!

The Famous Turkish Carpets

One day, while on an errand in the marketplace, Nurdan and Güldan hear chanting from a small house. "One blue, three red, one blue, two yellow," drones the voice.

Nurdan knows what is going on. "That is Ibrahim and his family working at the loom." They are making a carpet and will spend a lot of time on it so it will sell for a good price.

Turkey's carpets are valued worldwide. People seek them because of their durability and beauty. Their intricate, vivid designs look deceptively fragile, for these sturdy carpets can last over forty years. Small rugs, called *kilim*, are flat pieces of weaving. More valuable carpets are not woven but are made of tiny individual knots tied one at a time to the threads of the loom. The ends of the knots form the pile, or thickness, of the carpet. This is what makes it so comfortable to walk or sit on.

Women weaving a carpet on a loom.

Boys mending kilim, flat woven rugs.

Hundreds of years ago, nomadic tribes created the first knotted rugs. When they pitched their tents, they placed rugs and carpets on the earth for warmth and comfort. At first, these carpets were made by women and children working on a large loom laid on the ground. They used wool from their sheep, spinning it and then dyeing it with lovely colors made from plants.

Selecting rugs at an auction.

Later, when tribes settled in villages, they continued making carpets their customary way, but they set the loom upright so it was easier to work on. Sometimes entire families earn their living making carpets, using traditional designs passed down for hundreds of years. In some towns, rug making supports many people. It may take four or five people weeks, sometimes even months, to make a large carpet.

Ibrahim's family has finished the carpet. Now they will wash it in the traditional way. First the carpet is kneaded by hand to get rid of the stiffness; then it is thrown into a stream of running water. There Ibrahim and his sons scrub the carpet, scuffing it with their bare feet. Finally the carpet is laid in the sun to dry. Now it is ready to be sent to market where it will be auctioned — sold at the highest price rug dealers will pay. Most of the rugs and carpets purchased at the auction will be sent to other countries for people to buy.

Fruit for sale at the base of a rock pinnacle.

The Market

The sights and smells of Nevshehir's market delight Nurdan and Güldan alike. Besides the usual stores, many stalls appear for the day. Men and women sell their goods.

The girls stop at boxes of fruits and vegetables. Nurdan chooses some eggplants with great care and then selects tomatoes. Their errand for Mother is done, so they can wander about before going home. They pass a juice seller with his tank on his back. They sniff with pleasure as they pass the stall selling baked lamb wrapped in bread. At the roasted chestnut stand, Nurdan buys a bag. "Mother said we may have a treat," she says to Güldan. Sharing the bag, the sisters continue to stroll.

A juice seller.

Lamb baking on a spit.

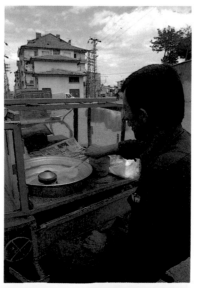

Lower left: Roasting chestnuts.

Lower right: Making cotton candy.

It is common in the market-place to see descendants of Arabs, Persians, and Europeans. Here is a blue-eyed woman with her arms full of dyed wool yarn. There is a dark-eyed tribesman in town to sell some goats. For centuries, warriors and wanderers from Middle Eastern and European nations have come in waves over the Anatolian plateau. And today their descendants are Turks, like Nurdan and her family.

Nurdan likes to window-shop. Outside the video rental store, they read posters and argue cheerfully about what they would like to rent some day. They linger in front of the shoe store, looking over colorful sandals and telling each other which ones they want. Then they pass a boy selling pens and pencils on tables he has set up. They dodge around another boy with a big tray of bread for sale.

A boy sells pens and pencils.

Colorful sandals for sale at the shoe store.

Nurdan's family rents many videos here.

Sunset over Nevshehir. The ruins of an ancient fortress remain at the summit of the hill.

The family gathers to have the evening meal together.

Friends and family join in the dancing. Spectators sing and clap.

An Evening Party

When the family sits down to dinner, two special dishes appear: *ekmek*, a heavy bread, and *pilaf*, a rice dish. Tonight dinner includes green beans stewed with tomatoes and beef, lamb hamburgers, pickled green peppers, a yogurt drink, and tripe soup

Pilaf, tomatoes, stew, pickled peppers, and tripe soup.

Everyone likes sugar in their tea.

Fruit and nuts are popular desserts.

Lamb shish kebab, a typical Turkish dish.

After dinner, old friends come to visit — Mehmet and Sena and their children. They bring a gift of roasted nuts. Handan makes tea, and Necati offers Mehmet *raki*, a drink made of fermented grapes and aniseed, which tastes like licorice.

Mehmet begins tapping a rhythm with a spoon. Sena ties her scarf around her waist and begins a lively step. Mesgüre kicks off her shoes and joins Sena. The children rush to join in the fun as everyone begins to hum a tune. The evening passes too quickly for Nurdan. She loves the singing, the teasing, and the friendly laughter. But most of all, she loves the dancing.

FOR YOUR INFORMATION: Turkey

Official Name:
Türkiye Cumhuriyeti
(Turk-EE-yuh juhm-HUHR-ee-yeh-tee)
Republic of Turkey

Capital:
Ankara

History

The land we now call Turkey has a history going back over 4,500 years. Modern
Turkey is simply the most recent in a series of important nations and empires that
have existed on the Anatolia peninsula — or Asia Minor, as it was called for many
years. This area has long been a critical land and water link between Europe and
Asia. So it is not surprising that for centuries, people have wanted to govern this
strategic area.

Istanbul, Turkey's largest city, and the great bridge over the harbor called the Golden Horn.

Prehistoric People

The first people to live in what is now called Turkey were there during the Neolithic, or "New Stone Age," period. One settlement dates as early as 6600 BC. They lived in small villages of mud huts, raising crops, keeping animals, working with stone tools, and making pottery. In about 2500 BC, they began using copper.

The Hittites

The first major group in the area was the Hittites, who lived in the area from 1900 BC until 1200 BC. They were powerful warriors, who designed and made chariots and bronze weapons. They built a strong kingdom, eventually becoming merchants, statesmen, and metalworkers, perhaps the first to work in iron. They were also excellent sculptors, and had two kinds of writing. One, with triangle-shaped letters, is called cuneiform. Another, like Egyptian hieroglyphics, had picturelike letters of things they represented.

The Hittites had well-organized government and a detailed code of written law. Councils made up of nobles advised the kings, who also served as priests, and governors appointed by kings ran the provinces. Courts were enlightened for that time. For instance, persons convicted of thievery were not jailed, tortured, or killed; they were ordered to repay victims.

The Hittites became a people with a great empire. Only mighty Egypt could resist them. Because neither side could defeat the other, the Hittite king Hattusili III finally made peace with the Egyptian pharaoh Ramses II in 1260 BC. But 60 years later, the Hittite Empire fell before a series of invasions by the Sea Peoples, several tribes of invaders who sailed over the Aegean Sea. They conquered various parts of Asia Minor and squabbled with one another for centuries. To this day, ruins left by these empires dot the landscape. In the ninth century BC, one tribe, the Phrygians, conquered the others. They adopted much of the Hittite system of government and became architects, builders, ironworkers, and artisans.

Persians, Greeks, and Romans

In the sixth century BC, the mighty Persian empire of Cyrus the Great began to conquer neighbors, including Asia Minor, and his descendants expanded the empire. But in 334 BC, the armies of the Greek leader Alexander the Great defeated the Persians. When Alexander died, his generals divided Anatolia among themselves. Wars, rebellions, and invasions plagued the region for decades.

Then, in 138 BC, the Romans invaded and extended their rule over all Asia Minor, although Greek culture survived in the cities. The area prospered under their rule. By AD 324, their emperor, Constantine I, moved the capital to Byzantium, renaming it Constantinople. Today, this city is called Istanbul; it is modern Turkey's largest city.

In AD 395, the Roman Empire was divided into two parts. Constantinople was the capital city of the Eastern part, known as the Byzantine Empire. Under Byzantine rulers, Christianity spread throughout Asia Minor. The people erected beautifully decorated churches. The empire became noted for its architecture, paintings, mosaics, textiles, and metalwork. Rulers encouraged astronomy, mathematics, and literature. But then, in the eleventh century, the Turks invaded Byzantium.

The Seljuk Turks

The Turks' conquest of this area helped lead to the Crusades, during which Christians tried to recapture the Holy Land. Then Seljuk Turks settled in Asia Minor, which included most of modern Turkey. As rulers of the first Turkish empire, they converted the people to Islam, established a system of government, and encouraged the arts.

Followers of Islam, the Seljuks defeated the Christian Byzantine army in 1071 and overran most of Asia Minor. Their mercenaries were Orghuz Turks, called Turkoman (Turkmen). The Seljuk reign peaked in the early 13th century, when they created the strongest state of the eastern Mediterranean. Today, their architecture can be seen in schools and mosques in many Anatolian cities. This architecture marks the beginning of Turkish art, an achievement to be elaborated on in later centuries.

The Ottoman Empire

When the Mongols, under Genghis Khan, invaded and conquered the Seljuks, the disorder that followed the invasion provided the opportunity for the Orghuz Turks to organize and to conquer the area. In time, they would become leaders of the Ottoman Empire. The founder of the Ottoman Empire was Osman, one of the Orghuz Turks, who began acquiring land by conquering Byzantine principalities. In 1326, Osman's son, Orkhan, conquered Bursa, the capital of the Byzantine province, and gained control of Byzantine systems of administration, finance, and military organization.

Ottoman sultans made several attempts to capture Constantinople, the capital of the Byzantine Empire. By 1453, Mehmet II, perhaps the most remarkable of the sultans, a poet and a scholar who had mastered six languages, was ready with a fleet, an enormous army, and huge cannons. The city was finally conquered as the result of a brilliant and unusual trick. He dragged his ships overland, across the inlet of the Bosporus called the Golden Horn, to the exposed side of the city. This event marks the official fall of the great Byzantine Empire. Mehmet, who knew the value of this strategically located city, rebuilt it as fast as resources allowed.

By the 16th century, the Ottomans had enormous power under Sultan Süleyman the Magnificent. They governed from the splendid Topkapi Palace, built in the 15th century and large enough to house 4,000 people. The empire eventually grew to an immense nation covering about 1,500,000 square miles (about 3,900,000 sq km), just under half the size of Canada or the United States.

The Ottomans drafted Christians into an elite infantry corps called the Janissaries, converted them to Islam, and gave them positions in the administration and army. Most governing was done by *kapikullari,* Muslims as well as Christian converts, who reported to the sultan. The goal of the government was to ensure the smooth working of the system, to arm the military, and to develop culture and religion.

The long reign of the Ottomans provided the stability a nation needs to encourage the arts. Süleyman heard of a young man named Sinan, who was said to be brilliant at building bridges and converting churches into mosques. In 1538, he made Sinan the royal architect. Under Süleyman, Sinan designed and supervised the building of mosques, schools, bridges, and fortifications. An enlightened ruler and man of culture, Süleyman encouraged other arts and sciences, too.

After Süleyman, the empire waned. A series of losses in wars in Europe forced the empire to sacrifice some border countries to neighbors like Russia. Conquered territories began rebelling, and the power of the sultans weakened. The empire had not developed its military and technological base as rapidly as Europeans had. By the early 19th century, people believed the Ottoman Empire, so mighty on a map, was really ready to collapse. They called it the "Sick Man of Europe."

The "Young Turks"

A group called the "Young Turks" became impatient with the sultan, Abd al-Hamid II, and overthrew him in 1909, putting a weaker leader in his place and thereby ruling the nation. In the next ten years, they modernized cities, farms, industries, and communications, weakened Islamic control of government, and improved the position of women.

Before they made more changes, World War I intervened; Turkey found itself fighting on the side of its closest ally and commercial partner, Germany. The Turkish army defeated the British and French at the famous battle at Gallipoli, in 1916, but elsewhere, against the Russian and the Arab-British forces, they did not fare well. In 1920, the exhausted empire submitted to the Treaty of Sèvres, which called for the partition of Turkey by British, French, Russian, and Greek forces.

Atatürk

But out of the ruins of the old empire arose a general whom many Turks consider their greatest leader — Mustafa Kemal. In 1919, Kemal began organizing a national movement and by 1922 had driven out or defeated the British, French, Russian, and Greek forces. A year later, he declared the independence of the new Republic of Turkey. For his sacrifices for his nation, the Turkish parliament later gave him the title Atatürk, which means "Father of the Turks."

As president, Atatürk loosened Islam's grip on government, replaced ancient Islamic laws with European-style legal codes, insisted that women and men have equal civil rights, encouraged Western dress, and urged everyone to educate themselves so they could lead the nation. He built schools throughout Turkey and replaced the old Arabic script, which few could master, with the simpler Roman alphabet. When Atatürk died in 1938, at age 57, Turkey mourned him deeply.

Modern Turkey — Potential and Problems

Atatürk's trusted colleague, Ismet Inönü, then became president. He kept Turkey neutral for most of World War II; only in February 1945 did they join the Allies; the war in Europe ended in May. In 1952, Turkey joined the North Atlantic Treaty Organization (NATO) and continues to honor its commitment; it has the second largest armed forces in the organization, second only to the US Army. During the 1950s, Turkey also joined the United Nations forces in the Korean War and lost many men.

After the wars, the government began developing industries, worked to stabilize its economy, and turned to social reforms. Then, in the 1970s and 1980s, a number of factors which by themselves might not unsettle a country combined to hamper progress. A war with Greeks erupted on Cyprus, poor budgeting caused debt and inflation, and the people became angry, so the government curbed freedom of speech. The government could not improve matters, and political squabbles resulted in terrorist acts. In 1980, the army had to step in to impose order.

Conditions stabilized in 1983. A new constitution and election brought the current prime minister, Turgut Özal, into office. While domestic problems remain, the nation has been able to avoid involvement in the Middle Eastern war and is a stable presence in the Mediterranean. It is content with its present borders and remains committed to Atatürk's philosophy, "Peace at home. Peace in the world."

Industry

Turkey continues to develop its economy, trading primarily with Iran, Iraq, and Saudi Arabia. It focuses on industry and plans to be a full member of the European Economic Community in the 1990s. Tourism, textile exports, and construction projects with the Organization of Petroleum Exporting Countries (OPEC) will help achieve this goal.

Besides manufacturing textiles, Turkey has food-processing industries and produces fertilizers, iron and steel, machinery, metal products, and pulp and paper products. The country exports cars, trucks, carpets, ceramics, cement, electronic equipment, fine leather, and household goods such as stoves and refrigerators. Major imports are dyes, rubber, petroleum, plastics, pharmaceuticals, and transport vehicles.

Population and Ethnic Groups

Over half of Turkey's 53 million people live in cities; the rest live in farming villages or other rural areas. About 85% of the people are Turks, originally from Central Asia and Mongolia's mountains and steppes. By the 11th century, some had settled in Anatolia and intermarried with the peoples who had come to the area earlier.

The Kurds are Turkey's largest ethnic minority — about 12% of the population, nomadic people who live with their sheep, cattle, and camels in southeastern Turkey and along the Soviet, Iranian, and Iraqi borders. Smaller ethnic groups include Arabs, Greeks, Armenians, Jews, Circassians, Georgians, and Muhacirs.

Language

About 90% of the Turks speak Turkish, the official language and a member of the Ural-Altaic group, which makes it related to Finnish and Hungarian. About 10% speak Kurdish or Arabic. A handful speak Greek or other languages. Many speak English or German because these languages are taught in the schools; German is more widely spoken because for years, many Turks have worked in Germany.

For centuries Turks used the Ottoman Turkish alphabet, written in Arabic characters. But it was so complicated that few used it well. Then, in 1928, Atatürk promoted the modern Roman alphabet and abolished use of the Ottoman alphabet.

Education

In 1923, when Atatürk assumed control, only 10% of the people could read and write. But when he replaced the Arabic script with the Roman alphabet, mastering written language became easier. Now over 70% of those over 15 can read. Much money for education goes to rural areas where schools and teachers are scarce. Children attend primary school for five years, and study a foreign language. Then they may attend three years of middle school and three of lise, after which they may go on to vocational school. Education is free through the lise level. Lise graduates who pass an exam may attend one of Turkey's 22 universities.

Turkey has declared April 23 World Children's Day, and every year celebrations occur on this day. Children from nearly every country participate in the festivities.

Religion

Turkey is the only Muslim nation to become a republic without an official religion. But about 98% of the people are Sunni Muslims, so reminders of Islam appear throughout the country, particularly in the many mosques, with their great minarets, or towers. Daily, men ascend these towers to call devout Muslims to prayers. People practice other faiths in Turkey, too. They include Judaism and Christian sects such as the Gregorian, Roman Catholic, and Greek Orthodox.

Celebrations bring together cousins, aunts, uncles, grandparents — the whole family.

Muslims consider their sacred book, the Koran, to be the message Allah, or God, sent to Muhammad, his Prophet. Islam takes its name from the Arabic word for submission or commitment to Allah. The "Five Pillars" guide devout Muslims. They are (1) openly declaring one's belief that there is only one God and Muhammad is his Prophet; (2) praying five times a day; (3) giving alms to the poor; (4) fasting during prescribed times; and (5) making a journey to the holy city, Mecca, in Saudi Arabia, at least once, if possible.

Music and Architecture

The Islamic religion prohibits representations of God and discourages using human figures as part of art. This may be the reason architecture has been one of Turkey's greatest art forms. Some of the most breathtaking buildings are the mosques.

Turkey's most famous architect, one of the world's great architects, was a man called Sinan the Architect. Born about 1489, Sinan designed or supervised the design of over 300 buildings, including mosques, tombs, palaces, municipal buildings, fountains, and aqueducts to carry water into and out of the city.

Sinan's Mosque of Süleyman the Magnificent is considered the most splendid of all imperial mosques in Istanbul. Standing on a hill, it is conspicuous by its great size, emphasized by its four minarets, each rising from one of the four corners of the courtyard. Inside, there are fine stained-glass windows, and the *mihrab*, or prayer niche, and the *mimber*, or pulpit, are of finely carved white marble. Adjoining the mosque are theological schools, a school of medicine, a soup kitchen, a hospice for the poor, and a Turkish bath. Also in Istanbul is the Blue Mosque. The main attraction of this mosque is its 21,043 blue Iznik tiles, painted predominantly with the ornate blue design that gives the mosque its name.

Turkey has enjoyed classical music from the West since Atatürk first introduced it, but its real treasure is its folk music, which has inspired such composers as Béla Bartók, Wolfgang Amadeus Mozart, and Ludwig van Beethoven. Troubadours called *ashiks* create songs spontaneously, strumming on stringed instruments called *saz*. Two dances done to folk music include the *zeybek* and the *horon*, lively dances done by men.

Government

Turkey has several political parties, but they compete according to two basic but different ideas. They either want to expand the government's role in many features of Turkish life or they want to reduce it. At 21, all Turkish citizens can vote.

Turkey's constitution provides for a president, who serves for seven years, a prime minister, a legislature called the Grand National Assembly, and a court system. The president, who is head of state and commander-in-chief of the armed forces, appoints the prime minister and can approve or veto laws passed by the Grand National Assembly, except laws concerning the budget. Since the president appoints important government officials, however, he has a great deal of power.

The prime minister runs the day-to-day activities of the government, assisted by a council of ministers. They report to the Grand National Assembly, a group with 400 members, elected to five-year terms. The Grand National Assembly selects the president and can pass bills into laws even if the president has vetoed them. It also has the power to make laws, declare war, and ratify treaties.

Local courts throughout Turkey take care of local civil and criminal trials, but people can appeal the decisions of these courts to the Court of Cassation. The Constitutional Court handles cases concerning the constitution. There is also a Military Court of Appeals. A High Council of Judges and Prosecutors, appointed by the president, supervises all these courts.

Local government is based on a system of provinces. The president selects a governor for each of the 67 provinces, and the people elect their own councils.

Natural Resources

Turkey is one of three nations providing the world's chromium ore; it also provides more than a third of the world's boron. Oil deposits remain in Turkey, but the country imports much oil to meet its energy needs. Coal remains abundant, but the government continues to develop hydroelectric power plants. Coal and iron ore deposits support a growing steel industry. Turkey also has a rich supply of meerschaum, a fine white clay used to make high-quality tobacco pipes.

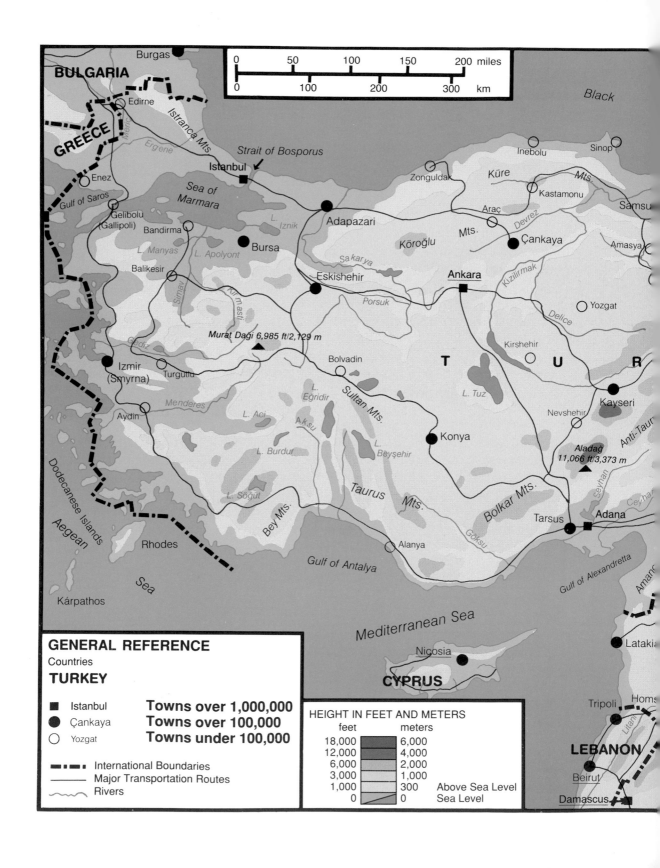

BULGARIA

Burgas

Edirne

GREECE

Enez

Gulf of Saros

Gelibolu
(Gallipoli)

Bandirma

Balikesir

Istranca Mts.

Ergene

Strait of Bosporus

Istanbul

Sea of
Marmara

L. Iznik

Adapazari

Bursa

L. Manyas

L. Apolyont

Eskishehir

Sakarya

Ankara

Porsuk

Murat Daği 6,985 ft/2,129 m

Izmir
(Smyrna)

Turgutlu

Aydin

Menderes

Balikesir

Simav

Kirmasti

Gediz

L. Eğridir

L. Aci

Aksu

Bolvadin

Sultan Mts.

L. Beyşehir

Konya

Nevshehir

Aladağ
11,066 ft/3,373 m

L. Burdur

L. Söğüt

Bey Mts.

Taurus   Mts.

Bolkar Mts.

Tarsus

Adana

Göksu

Alanya

Gulf of Antalya

Rhodes

Dodecanese Islands

Aegean

Sea

Kárpathos

Black

Inebolu

Sinop

Zonguldak

Küre

Kastamonu

Araç

Devrez

Samsu

Çankaya

Amasya

Köroğlu

Mts.

Kizilirmak

Yozgat

Delice

Kirshehir

T   U   R

L. Tuz

Kayseri

Anti-Taur

Seyhan

Ceyha

Gulf of Alexandretta

Aman

Mediterranean Sea

Nicosia

CYPRUS

Latakia

Tripoli

Homs

Litani

LEBANON

Beirut

Damascus

0	50	100	150	200 miles
0	100	200	300	km

GENERAL REFERENCE

Countries

TURKEY

■ Istanbul   **Towns over 1,000,000**

● Çankaya   **Towns over 100,000**

○ Yozgat   **Towns under 100,000**

▪—▪—▪ International Boundaries
—— Major Transportation Routes
〜〜 Rivers

HEIGHT IN FEET AND METERS

feet	meters	
18,000	6,000	
12,000	4,000	
6,000	2,000	
3,000	1,000	
1,000	300	Above Sea Level
0	0	Sea Level

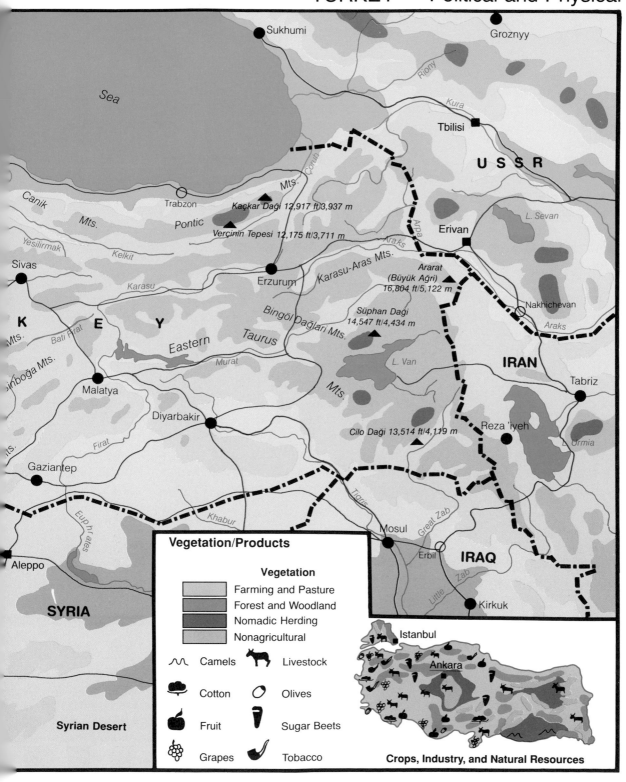

TURKEY — Political and Physical

Sukhumi

Groznyy

Rioni

Kura

Tbilisi

U S S R

Sea

Mts.

Çoruh

L. Sevan

Canik

Trabzon

Pontic

Kaçkar Daği 12,917 ft/3,937 m

Mts.

Yeşilirmak

Kelkit

Verçinin Tepesi 12,175 ft/3,711 m

Arpa

Erivan

Araks

Sivas

Karasu

Erzurum

Karasu-Aras Mts.

Ararat
(Büyük Ağri)
16,804 ft/5,122 m

Nakhichevan

K

E

Y

Mts.

Bati Firat

Araks

Bingöl Dağlari Mts.

Süphan Daği
14,547 ft/4,434 m

IRAN

inboğa Mts.

Eastern

Taurus

Murat

L. Van

Malatya

Tabriz

Mts.

Diyarbakir

Cilo Daği 13,514 ft/4,119 m

Reza 'iyeh

L. Urmia

Firat

Gaziantep

Euphrates

Tigris

Great Zab

Khabur

Mosul

Erbil

IRAQ

Aleppo

Little Zab

Kirkuk

SYRIA

Vegetation/Products

Vegetation

Farming and Pasture
Forest and Woodland
Nomadic Herding
Nonagricultural

∿∿ Camels   Livestock

Cotton   Olives

Fruit   Sugar Beets

Grapes   Tobacco

Syrian Desert

Istanbul

Ankara

Crops, Industry, and Natural Resources

Land

About 3% of Turkey lies in Europe, separated from Asian Turkey by the Bosporus and Dardanelles straits and the Sea of Marmara. Known as Eastern Thrace, this area is all that remains of Turkey's Ottoman Empire in Europe. Thrace's fertile grasslands make it a valuable farming and grazing area. The rest of Turkey lies in Asia and is often called Asia Minor, or Anatolia. It has three main regions: the Aegean coast, the central Anatolian plateau, and the eastern highlands.

The central Anatolian plateau, with its rim of rugged, towering mountains, is the largest region. This area receives little rain, but it falls all year, so grass and grain grow well. Nomadic herders tend goats and sheep and farm in the river valleys. Many of the limestone mountains contain caves and underground streams. Small glaciers and shallow salt lakes dot the countryside. Part of the plateau has a landscape of volcanic tuff eroded into intriguing shapes like mushrooms, towers, and needles.

The eastern highlands have both high, rugged mountains and plains where herds can graze but few crops will grow. Earthquakes shake this unstable area. The highest mountain is Mt. Ararat, over 16,800 feet (5,100 m) high. Tradition says that this is the place Noah's ark landed after the flood. Two great rivers, the Tigris and the Euphrates, rise in these highlands.

The northern and southern coasts have narrow strips of fertile land. Forests line the slopes of the mountains separating these coasts from the central highlands. The Republic of Cyprus lies 40 miles (64 km) south of Turkey in the Mediterranean Sea. Along the Aegean coast, many Greek islands lie very close to Turkey's shore, the closest being less than two miles (3 km) away. Because of their proximity, Greeks and Turks have had a history of hostile relations concerning land.

Agriculture

About 52% of working Turks are farmers, but they cultivate only about a third of the land. Farms are small and methods still inefficient; only in the past 20 years have tractors become common. But Turkey produces enough food for its own needs and for export. Production rises, of course, wherever farmers use machinery, fertilizers, and irrigation, and breed animals for particular qualities.

The mild climate supports several crops in two major fertile areas, the coasts and the plateau. Productive farmlands are near the coasts of the Black, Aegean, and Mediterranean seas. This land produces grapes, olives, and citrus and other fruits. Crops grown and exported are tobacco, sugar beets, fruits, tea, potatoes, and nuts. Inland, the great Anatolian plateau is the grain-growing region, producing barley, oats, rye, corn, and wheat. Turkey is sixth in world production of cotton.

Everyone prizes Angora goats, grown for their long, silky hair, called mohair. Sheep provide meat and wool, and goats and cattle provide meat and hides. Cattle also serve as draft animals. Other livestock raised on farms are horses, donkeys, water buffalo, camels, and poultry.

Climate

Turkey enjoys a pleasant climate. Most of Thrace and the Aegean and Mediterranean coasts have mild, wet winters, with an average January temperature of 48°F (9°C). Temperatures in the hot, dry summers average 84°F (29°C).

The central Anatolian plateau gets about half the rain of the coast, and it has colder winters and cooler summers; its average summer temperature is 73°F (23°C). And the eastern highlands have long, cold winters. The area is wetter than the plateau, mostly because of snow. In the mountains, winters are harsh, with temperatures sometimes going below -40°F (-40°C). This area supports several ski resorts.

The famous hot spring area of Pamukkale, its rocks coated with minerals.

Rainfall amounts also vary widely. The Mediterranean and Aegean coasts get about 20 to 30 inches (51 to 76 cm) of rain a year, about the amount recorded by the Midwest in the US. But areas near the Black Sea can get over 100 inches (about 250 cm) of rain annually.

Currency

The monetary unit of Turkey is the Turkish *lira*, or TL. Paper money is printed in denominations of 5, 10, 20, 50, 100, 500, 1,000, 5,000, and 10,000 lira, and coins in denominations of 1, 2 1/2, 5, 10, and 100 lira. Like all currencies world-wide, the lira's value fluctuates. In 1989, about 2,040 TL equaled one US dollar. Inflation causes great losses in the lira's value, so the government tries to make its value more stable.

Sports and Recreation

Turks enjoy sports, as spectators and as participants. Contests and games allow players to prove physical or mental abilities. Some men have "cockfights," in which two players imitate fighting roosters, each hopping on one foot. Friends circle the "roosters" and cheer. Other popular sports are soccer and basketball. Wrestling, a traditional sport, has won Turkey Olympic medals and other titles.

Other Turkish games stress cooperation over competition. They combine elements of tag, guessing games, and hide-and-seek. Children and adults excitedly run, hop, chant, and shout. Instead of emphasizing winning and losing, they focus on fun. Most people also enjoy folk dancing, and each region has special dances, which they do to traditional instruments and singing. In good weather, Turks like to picnic, and during the summer vacation months, they crowd the beaches.

Ankara

Istanbul was Turkey's capital until 1923, when Atatürk moved it to Ankara, partially because of Ankara's central location and the loyalty of its citizens during the war of liberation. It was little more than a small town then, although it was over 4,000 years old. Now it is a modern city with a population of about 2,251,000.

Modern Ankara still echoes its rich past. The Temple of Augustus, only partly intact, bears the last will of that great Roman emperor. Engraved on bronze almost 2,000 years ago, it has been immensely valuable to scholars. The Column of Julian stands in memory of the year AD 362, when the Roman emperor Julian visited the city. Other ruins are the Baths of Caracalla, which reveal the outlines of the large, ancient pool, and the Citadel, or Hisar, ancient Anatolia's mightiest stronghold. Built by the Galatians and fortified by the Romans and the Seljuk Turks, this fortress bears the scars of centuries of warfare. Mosques about the city testify to the religious fervor that created both the Seljuk and Ottoman empires.

In contrast to the ancient, however, is the modern city built by Atatürk. Drawn by his personality, thousands of homeless Turks took up his call to Ankara. Under his watchful eye, they built a capital of spacious, well-planned streets and houses. Atatürk, who died in 1938, was buried in a great mausoleum, or tomb, high on a hill, with tall columns and interior walls lined with rich marbles and mosaics. In addition to the Museum of Anatolian Civilizations and the Atatürk Museum, the city is also the home of Turkey's government buildings, the state opera and ballet, and countless modern factories, schools, and homes.

Istanbul

A city of six million, Istanbul lies on the Bosporus, with most of its area in Europe. It contains the Golden Horn, an excellent natural harbor, and is a strategic and wealthy city. When the Greeks founded the city in the seventh century BC, they called it Byzantium. For over 1,000 years, many nations in the Mediterranean fought over it. When, in AD 324, Constantine I made the city the capital of the

Roman Empire, he named it after himself — Constantinople. Eleven centuries and many wars later, it was the capital of the Byzantine Empire and a center of trade and culture. In 1204, the Crusaders gained control; then, in 1453, the Ottomans conquered the city, ruling for hundreds of years and adorning the city with grand buildings. After World War I, the Allies moved in. But in 1923, Atatürk roused the Turks to regain control. In 1930 the city became Istanbul.

One reminder of this incredible past is Hagia Sophia, built by Christians in the sixth century AD, and made into a mosque in AD 1453. Only traces of Hagia Sophia's glory remain, but with its four tall minarets and massive dome, the building still thrills visitors. Now, it is a museum of Byzantine art. Other revered buildings in Istanbul are the great Süleymaniye and Mihrimah mosques and the Seraglio, the palace buildings and grounds of the Ottoman sultans.

Istanbul also has modern delights. Old walls have made way for modern buildings. Tourists enjoy bathing beaches and new air-conditioned hotels. Vehicles whiz past trendy stores on wide streets. The new complements the traditional.

Turks in North America

The number of Turks who have immigrated to North America in the last ten years has fluctuated. From about the 1960s to the 1980s, economic problems caused unrest in Turkey; on two occasions, military governments stepped in. In 1982, the new president assumed office. A more stable Turkey may have affected the number of Turks who emigrated. From 1978 to 1982, in Canada, the number jumped from 192 to a high of 838. But after the election, the number fell to 297. The number immigrating to the US doubled — from about 1,600 in 1978 to nearly 3,000 in 1982 — after which it dropped to 1,700 by 1986. The numbers of people migrating to work or study followed a similar pattern, rising in the early 1980s and dropping thereafter. Most Turks go to Chicago, Atlanta, Houston, Dallas, and Los Angeles, cities with jobs and universities. Students usually return to Turkey, but professionals tend to remain in North America.

Glossary of Useful Turkish Terms

anne (UHN-neh) .... mother
baba (BUH-buh) .... father
cadde (JUH-deh) .... street, avenue
çocuk (CHO-juk) .... children
ev (ehv) .... house
pide (PEE-deh) .,................................ a food similar to pizza
sabah (SUH-buh) .... morning
simit (see-MEET) .... bread; a cross between a bagel and a pretzel

More Books About Turkey

Constantinople: City of the Golden Horn. Jacobs (Harper Jr.)
Eliph: Child of Turkey. Bruni (Texart)
Islam. Barlow (David & Charles)
The Land and People of Turkey. Spencer (Harper Jr.)
A Turkish Afternoon. Bennett (David & Charles)

Things to Do — Research Projects

Over the centuries, many peoples have crossed Turkey in search of adventure, riches, or a safe place to live. Today it remains a strategic nation in the world. Neighbor to both the Soviet Union and the warring nations of Iran and Iraq, Turkey has avoided major conflicts and maintained an active role in NATO. As you learn more about Turkey's crucial role in history, keep in mind the importance of current facts. Some of the projects that follow need up-to-date information, so use current newspapers and magazines for information. Two library publications will help you find recent articles on many topics such as those listed below:

Readers' Guide to Periodical Literature
Children's Magazine Guide

1. From the sixteenth to the nineteenth century, the Ottoman Empire dominated the Mediterranean region. Read more about this immensely powerful empire.

2. Turkey is surrounded on three sides by seas: the Aegean, the Black, and the Mediterranean. Learn how the seas have affected Turkey's economy and history.

3. If you were a Turkish child, what foods would your family commonly eat at meals? Read about agriculture in Turkey and the kinds of fruit, vegetables, grains, and livestock produced in this land.

More Things to Do — Activities

1. Learn more about the religious holidays of Islam. With a group of friends or classmates, plan a religious festival. Why is this holiday important? What foods are served? What rituals occur?

2. If you would like a pen pal from Turkey, write to these people:

International Pen Friends
P.O. Box 290065
Brooklyn, NY 11229

Worldwide Pen Friends
P.O. Box 39097
Downey, CA 90241

Tell where you want your pen pal to be from and include your name and address.

Index